Landscape
QUILTS

with

Kathy McNeil

American Quilter's Society

www.AmericanQuilter.com

Located in Paducah, Kentucky, the American Quilter's Society (AQS) is dedicated to promoting the accomplishments of today's quilters. Through its publications and events, AQS strives to honor today's quiltmakers and their work and to inspire future creativity and innovation in quiltmaking.

EXECUTIVE EDITOR: KIMBERLY H. TETREV
SENIOR EDITOR: LINDA BAXTER LASCO
PROOFREADER: ADRIANA FITCH
ILLUSTRATIONS: SARAH BOZONE
GRAPHIC DESIGN: SARAH BOZONE
COVER DESIGN: MICHAEL BUCKINGHAM
QUILT PHOTOGRAPHY: CHARLES R. LYNCH
SCENERY PHOTOGRAHY: BRUCE MCNEIL

Additional copies of this book may be ordered from the American Quilter's Society, PO Box 3290, Paducah, KY 42002-3290, or online at www.AmericanQuilter.com.

Text © 2015, Author, Kathy McNeil
Artwork © 2015, American Quilter's Society

American Quilter's Society
PO Box 3290 • Paducah, KY 42002-3290
Fax 270-898-1173 • email: orders@AQSquilt.com

Library of Congress Cataloging-in-Publication Data

McNeil, Kathy (Quiltmaker)
   Landscape quilts with Kathy McNeil / by Kathy McNeil.
      pages cm
   Includes bibliographical references and index.
   ISBN 978-1-60460-179-4 (alk. paper)
   1. Quilting–Patterns. 2. Quilts–Themes, motives. 3. Landscapes in art.
   I. Title.
   TT835.M4724 2015
   746.46–dc23
                              2015007128

Dedication and Acknowledgments

To my one true love, Bruce McNeil, whose kindness and generosity inspire me every day.

To Geri Parker, who believed in me and set me on this teaching journey.

With gratitude to Jane Lovett at Falls Mills, 134 Falls Mills Road, Belvidere, Tennessee, for giving a home to my sixty-third quilt. She allowed me to use her historic old mill as the inspiration for the FALL pattern.

Contents

The CD contains all your patterns. There are two ways to print them:
A. On 8½" x 11" sheets OR
B. Full size on one sheet from a commercial printer

Version A: You may print them out on your home computer in 8½" x 11" sheets. Tape the sheets together using the registration marks.

Version B: You may also take your CD to your local copy center. Tell them the exact measurement, listed below, along with the page number the full size pattern can be found on for the pattern you want printed. Tell them to click on the Full Size Pattern For Commercial Printer and it will take them to the page they will need to print.

Page numbers are:
Spring - pg. 17
Summer - pg. 29
Fall - pg. 44
Winter - pg. 59

The size of the page you need to tell them to print is:
Winter and Spring 28½" x 21½"
Summer and Fall 21½" x 23"
This size will give you a ½" white space on all sides of the pattern.

Check all pattern measurements before beginning.

Introduction

Mother Nature provides me with daily inspiration and more quilt ideas than I can make in a lifetime. I just finished my sixty-sixth quilt inspired by a dream trip to Provence, France. It was early summer and the poppies danced across the fields like butterflies.

Poppies of Provence 40" x 41", made by the author

Every season brings its own gifts of color, sound, and textures. Quilts rotate at my house, matching the season or the holiday, I hope these four quilts will add to your anticipation and joy of each season.

> Spring passes and one remembers one's innocence.
> Summer passes and one remembers one's exuberance.
> Autumn passes and one remembers one's reverence.
> Winter passes and one remembers ones's perseverance.
>
> Yoko Ono

These patterns are meant to be photo realistic. They are not stylized, easy, abstract landscapes. More details, shading, and textural differences are apparent in realistic looking landscapes. I have included hints for adding depth and perspective to all four patterns. You have all the basic landscape ingredients—trees, mountains, streams, seascape, etc.—to learn how to create a basic, realistic looking landscape.

This pattern book will help you build your confidence in the joys of landscape quilting.

When you complete these patterns, you will have the experience to begin creating your own favorite scenes.

If you are new to appliqué, landscape quilting, or need more help with assembly, painting on fabric, using sheers, learning multiple appliqué techniques, and free motion quilting see:
Learning Landscapes in the resource section (page 61).

This is a one hour and 55 minute DVD that shows you step-by-step how each quilt in this book was made. It includes:

- Choosing fabrics for landscapes to create dimension and form.

- How to shade with fabric paint crayons to add highlights and shadows.

- Multiple ways to appliqué and how to handle those complex shapes.

In the video, you can watch me turn an edge or paint on fabric as if you were looking right over my shoulder. No movement will be uncertain. You will feel like we are working in your studio on these patterns together.

1

2

Tree Tops

12

11

13

1

4

3

7

lawn

General Instructions
The Patterns

Traditional appliqué is layered. Does this piece go behind or on top of OR behind another piece? If it goes under, a small extension of the bottom shape will be needed to appliqué the top shape to. Cut out extensions on all the pieces that will partly fall under another pattern piece. See the dotted lines for examples. Without the overlaps, all pieces would need to fit together like puzzle pieces. Our eyes and hands are not as precise as a laser pattern cutter.

Pattern sample. The dotted lines indicate where the completed shapes fall under another piece. (Not all lines are drawn in because it could get very confusing as you can see from the drawing.)

Numbers suggest the order of layering. The shapes I drew are suggested shapes! They indicate the maximum size a piece should be. It is more important to fussy-cut around small scale foliage prints, if you can find them, than to use my generic shapes for trees, bushes, etc. I often fussy cut shapes from a particular print and then collage them together until they cover the approximate shape or size shown in the pattern. Remember, the joy of doing landscapes is that every tree, every bush, and every snow bank in the world is different. Relax, this is not like making a Mariner's Compass. Cut out OR fill in the approximate shapes indicated in the pattern with the best possible choice of fabrics you can find. If your tree is a bit shorter than my tree it will be fine! *If you have a small hole, add another bush!*

20

Use a Plastic Overlay

Prior to beginning your quilt project, trace the entire pattern onto clear plastic. Use this as your position aide. Laminated plastic or upholstery vinyl work well.

Position the overlay on top of the background. As you add pieces to your composition, slide the completed shape under the traced position aide to check its placement before appliquéing to your background.

Use Your Favorite Appliqué Method

I use multiple techniques to do the appliqué work in my pieces. There are pros and cons to all techniques. Fusing can be a challenge because of the spatial issues involved in working with a mirror image. The process is faster but the feel of the final quilt will be stiffer. Fused pieces can lift up over time and the edges will fray more unless they are finished with machine appliqué Handwork can be a challenge for those with arthritis in their fingers.

A lot more loft and dimension can be created from turning the edges in your appliquéd shapes than with fusing. The quilts will feel like quilts when you are done. Many people like machine appliqué. The edges are turned under and the piece secured to the background with a small narrow zigzag stitch or blanket stitch.

Raw Edge/Fused Appliqué

Fusing to the back side of your fabrics requires you to use the mirror image to trace your template shapes onto your fusible product. If you choose to use this technique, flip and trace your pattern from the back OR simply turn your plastic overlay to the back side and trace your shapes from this mirror image onto your fusible product. You may choose to fuse your entire project OR buy just enough Lite Steam-a-Seam 2® to complete the smaller more difficult pieces.

Lite Steam–a-Seam 2® is my favorite fusible product. It is tacky enough that you can finger press your pieces into position, allowing you to audition your fabric choices and make exchanges before your heat set them into position with your iron.

Use rubbing alcohol to wipe your clear plastic clean. It can now be used for another project.

Kathy McNeil 🪡 Landscape Quilts with Kathy McNeil

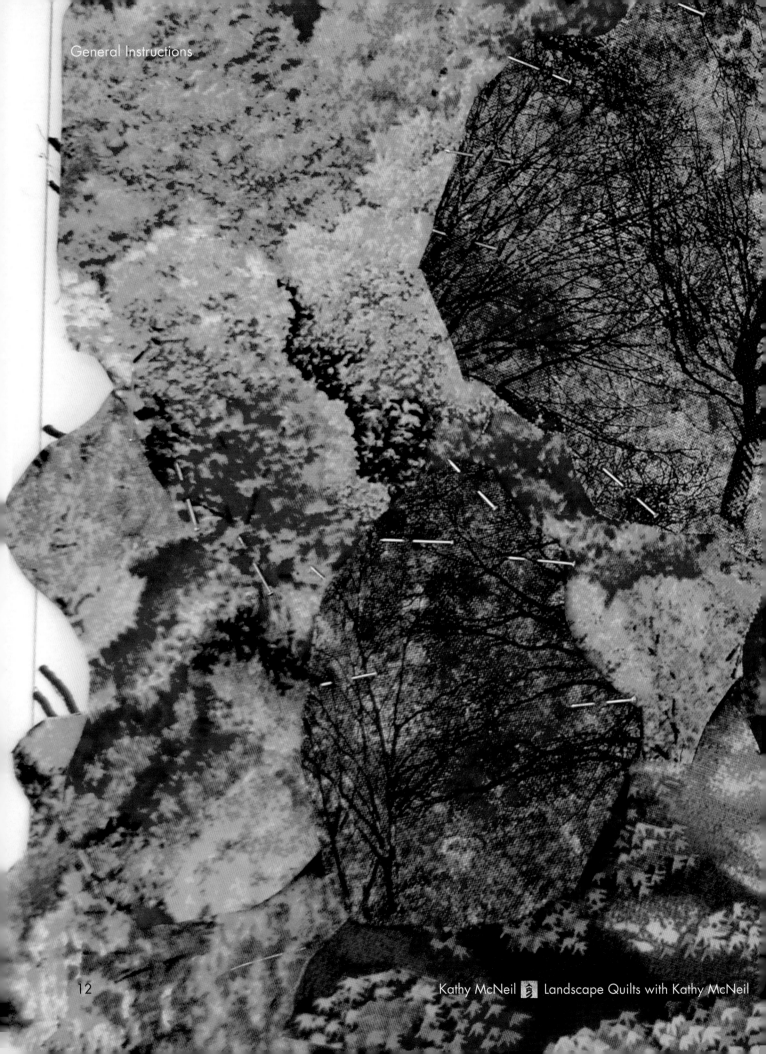

Kathy McNeil 🐦 Landscape Quilts with Kathy McNeil

Turned/Finished Edge Appliqué

Cut out each template shape with a ³⁄₁₆" seam allowance. DO NOT CUT UP YOUR PRINTED PATTERN! Remember to add in those overlap extensions that go behind other pieces.

Make templates for each pattern piece using your preferred material—Apliquick®™ stabilizer, tracing paper, freezer paper, etc.

Use your preferred hand appliqué needle and threads. Trim away multiple layers from behind (for example, the sky or water) as needed.

Template Materials for Cutting Out Pattern Pieces

Trace easy shapes onto tracing paper and then turn under with sizing or starch. Turn the edges of more complex shapes with the Apliquick®™ stabilizer method. Watch the free video on my website www. kathymcneilquilts.com to learn how to turn your edges with this method. It is my absolute favorite way to handle shapes that need to be more precise. Tiny complex shapes can be fused or needle turned.

Border Finishes

Add 1" wide inside border strips in the appropriate lengths. They will finish to ½".

Add 2½" outer borders. They will finish to 2".

An alternative border is offered in the Winter Pattern instructions (page 58).

Kathy McNeil 🌿 Landscape Quilts with Kathy McNeil

Choosing Fabrics for Landscape Quilts

Batiks *without* a strong visual motif and small scale prints work best for pictorial work. Solids do not work. They tend to flatten your composition.

Use multiple prints or the parts of a batik with some variation in value or color to add visual interest and the illusion of highlights or shading. Prints that are specifically made to appear like bark or distant trees are helpful. Landscape panels can be useful for fussy cutting specific features like trees or shrubbery from.

Kathy McNeil ❦ Landscape Quilts with Kathy McNeil

Remember everything gets more muted in color and grayer in value as it recedes toward the background. Choosing your fabrics accordingly will greatly enhance the sense of depth and perspective in your work. Some fabrics will flip to the "wrong side." The print will appear more muted on the back.

painted on top. Allow the fabric to dry and heat set with your iron on a cotton setting. There is no change to the "hand" or feel of the fabric which makes these ideal for hand appliqué work.

Derwent™ Inktense™ pencils work well for drawing

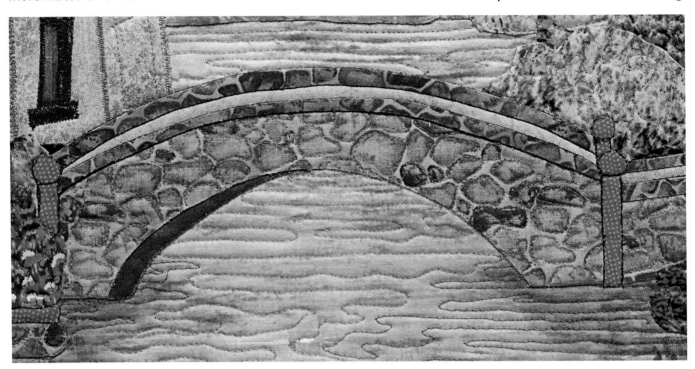

I often flip my fabrics to use in the background. For example, see the bridge in the Spring pattern.

I used the back side of the fabric to get that more muted, farther away look. The top railing is the "right side" with a brighter more saturated color. There is enough contrast in value between the front and back sides to visually separate the railing (front side) from the entire bridge (back side), giving it all a more detailed and realistic look.

Art Supplies

Consider using art media supplies to enhance the color, highlights or shadows to your selected fabric pieces. My favorite is Neocolor® II water color paint crayons. I love how the color disburses softly across the fabric.

That watercolor effect is often exactly what you are looking for. The paint crayons are easy to use and do not dry out. (They are already in crayon form.) The paint is transparent, so the print or texture you chose for this pattern piece will show through. The colors heat set permanently without the need of a fabric medium

more specific lines or in coloring in controlled shapes. Inks are a little more opaque. Not as much of your print will show through. Be sure to paint over the ink with fabric medium. Allow the fabric to dry and heat set permanently with your iron. The fabric medium does change the feel of the fabric. That's why I like Neocolor® better. Prismacolor® Prism Color Pencils also need to be painted over with fabric medium.

You can find the paint crayons, Inktense™ pencils and instructions for use on fabric in my web store www. kathymcneilquilts.com.

The *Learning Landscapes* DVD has an entire segment where you can watch me painting on fabrics for landscape quilting.

Binding

All the quilts were finished with a 2½" straight-of-grain binding. I used fabric to match the darker outer borders. In the Winter quilt, I chose to use one of the prints used in the pieced border.

Kathy McNeil 🖋 Landscape Quilts with Kathy McNeil

General Supplies for All Four Patterns

Basic sewing supplies.
- Fine point Sharpie® marker
- Clear plastic overlay for tracing your project. (You can reuse the same piece of plastic by wiping the "permanent" marker off with rubbing alcohol)
- Template material for all your shapes. This will depend on whether you plan to fuse or turn your edges. See the descriptions under appliqué methods (page 10).
- Spray sizing or spray starch.
- Glue pen or stick
- Hand appliqué needles or supplies if you choose to hand appliqué. Threads to match.
- Machine appliqué threads to match fabrics.
- Tear-away stabilizer for thread work or machine embroidery enhancements.
- Art media like Neocolor® II paint crayons or Ink tense pencils. Fabric medium if you want to use Inktense™ or Prismacolor® Prism Color Pencils.

Combined Fabric List

These fabrics can be used for more than one pattern.

Sky (for SPRING, SUMMER, and FALL) ¾ yard.

Water (for SPRING, SUMMER, and FALL). ⅔ yard.

Landscape bushes (for SPRING, SUMMER, and FALL) 2 – 3 landscape panels with a variety of small scale bushes, or quarter yard pieces of small scale floral bushes ½ - ¾ yard total.

Rock walls (for the bridge in WINTER, the lighthouse rock wall in SUMMER, and water wheel supports in FALL) ¼ yard

Green lawn (for SPRING and SUMMER) ¼ yard

House (for SPRING and FALL) ¼ yard

Red roof, trim (for SPRING and FALL houses and stripes for the lighthouse) ¼ yard

Spring

SPRING, 32½" x 25½", made by the author

Fabric Suggestions

The Stonehenge line of fabrics works beautifully for architectural features like buildings. Be sure to choose lighter fabrics for the sides of your chateau. The walls facing you will need to be slightly darker in value. Shading helps create perspective in your buildings. Small scale rock or brick fabrics can be used for the two rock walls. Using a variety of prints with slight differences in value or details will add dimension and form to your foliage and garden areas. Prints used in the foreground flower bushes should be larger in scale and more saturated in color than foliage in the mid ground and back ground. Collage together your bushes from fussy cut nature prints that you like.

Remember the **shapes on the pattern are suggested shapes!** They indicate the maximum size a clump should be. You can always break these generic bush shapes into smaller shapes. Collage your fussy-cut shapes together from several prints until they cover the approximate shape size or area shown in the pattern. The tree line is a suggested shape. If you have great trees to fussy cut from, just use the shape in your print.

The easiest way to create shading in the water on both sides of the bridge is by using the fabric paint crayons (see the General Instructions, page 16). Overdye darker color onto your lighter water fabric along both sides around rock walls as indicated on the pattern. Add dots of reflected color from the flowers into the water. Consider painting in little ripple lines to indicate water flow.

Kathy McNeil Landscape Quilts with Kathy McNeil

Fabrics Needed

- ½ yard for the sky
- ¼ yard for the water
- 1" x 6" muted green for the distant riverside (It should almost blend into the sky.)
- 2-3 quarter yards of distant tree fabrics, one lighter in value than the others (A variety of prints will be better than a single half-yard if you can find them.)
- Fat eighth of dark green for the tall, skinny trees
- 4 - 6 scraps from quarter yards of small-scale shrubbery for landscape bushes. (Variety adds interest to your landscape.)
- ¼ yard for the foreground flowering bush (Be sure scale is small enough. The flowers should be no more than ½" wide. You can use a green bush fabric and fuse small flowers cut from a small scale flower print on top of the green bush fabric to create your own flowering bush.)
- ¼ yard of small-scale rock fabric (Try to find a print that will flip to a usable muted side. Use the muted side for the bridge and the darker, right side for railings and foreground rock walls.)
- Various scraps for poles, tops, and darker sides of rock walls
- 2" x 8" light green for the lawn

- ¼ yard for the walls of the house
- Look for darker areas from your batik or Stonehenge prints for the shaded sides. If your print does not include a darker area, you will need to buy an additional quarter yard, darker in value, OR use your fabric paint crayons to overdye an 8" x 9" section slightly darker in color.
- Medium blue scraps for the windows
- Optional - Organza for reflective quality over windows. Make sure you can iron it with a lower heat setting!
- 9" x 9" reddish brown for the roof and trim
- 2" x 2" brown for the chimney
- ¼ yard of tear-away stabilizer for machine appliqué of organza over windows.
- ⅜ yard inner border and binding (Use a color that will help pop the colors used in the quilt interior)
- ⅜ yard outer border
- ⅜ yard binding
- You may want to just increase the fabric used for the outer border strips.
- ¾ yard backing
- 38" x 30" batting

Sewing Instructions

1. Trace your entire pattern onto a clear plastic overlay (page 10).

2. Cut a 13" x 29" rectangle of sky fabric and a 9" x 29" rectangle of water fabric. Join to make a 29" x 21½" rectangle for your background.

3. Layer the trees behind the house as numbered or fussy cut your tree fabric to follow the printed tree clumps in your chosen fabric. Collage these together following the suggested tree line and drawn shapes. If your fabric printed images are smaller than the pattern, just cut additional smaller shapes until the tree area is complete.

4. Appliqué the distant riverside shore strip in place. Align the bottom of this piece over the seam between sky and water. Your house and the landscaping on the right side will layer on top of it.

Kathy McNeil ◗ Landscape Quilts with Kathy McNeil

5. Begin assembling the house making sure to shade as discussed. Personalize your house! Add a window box of flowers at the back. Add a cross to make it an old church or monastery. Layer silk organza over the darker parts of windows to create a glass-like sheen. (Satin stitch over the edges to secure them.) Add more windows or a door. If your house is hand appliquéd, consider using a satin stitch to outline your windows. Be sure to put a tear-away stabilizer behind your quilt top when doing the satin stitching.

Special Note on Fusing

If you are fusing your house to the background, mark the outside edges of house onto the background with chalk pencil. Trim away the bulky sky and water seam line from under the house area <u>inside</u> your chalk line by ¼" on both sides. Cover the area with a small piece of interfacing or muslin before fusing the house in position over the back ground. Now your house will lie nice and flat instead of having a ridge across it from the seam line. Consider machine appliquéing the edges after fusing with a flat narrow zigzag stitch and matching thread to prevent fraying.

6. The drawn shapes of the landscape gardens on the right are the suggested maximum size for each clump of foliage. Feel free to fussy cut from interesting landscape prints and collage together until the area is covered. Spring should have lots of colorful flowering bushes and multiple shades of green. Layer as indicated by the numbers. **Be sure to leave the edge of the foliage free until the bridge is done and layered under bushes.** Add the two large, darkest in value green tree shapes.

7. The ends for the bridge should fall under the bushes on both sides. Numbers 15 and above should be added after your bridge is finished. Make sure the shaded, underside of the bridge is darker in value. Add the roadbed behind the bridge front. The railing falls on top. The railings should also be darker. If your bridge fabric can flip to a lighter back side, use that for the front of the bridge and the darker "right" side for the railings.

8. Begin landscaping in front of your house. The rock wall can be the darker, more colorful side of the same fabric you used for the bridge. Collage together the basic area with a variety of prints. Add a dark tree shape over wall of the house.

9. Shade your water using fabric paint crayons or cut skinny strips from darker colored fabrics and fuse them on top of your water.

10. For turned edges, trim all background from behind pictorial elements.

Finishing

Square up and trim to measure 27½" x 20½". Be sure to square parallel to the horizon line of the sky and water.

For the inner border, cut two strips 1" x 20½" and add to sides. Cut 2 strips 1" x 28½" and add to the top and bottom. Trim as needed.

For the outer border, cut 2 strips 2½" x 21½" and add to the sides. Cut 2 strips 2½" x 32½" and add to top and bottom.

Optionally, add pictorial images to your border.

Quilting your Quilt

Layer the quilt top, batting, and backing and pin baste together about every 3".

Begin by outline quilting all the major shapes. Go back and quilt within the shapes, adding texture that will enhance the visual look of the image; for example, pebbling around the stones in your rock wall.

Be consistent with the density of your free-motion quilting across the entire quilt top.

Pattern sample for SPRING. Full size pattern on CD.
Printed pattern must measure 27½" x 20½". Please check your printed pattern before you begin.

Summer

SUMMER, 27" x 25½", made by the author

Kathy McNeil 🪆 Landscape Quilts with Kathy McNeil

Fabric Suggestions

The Stonehenge line of fabrics or batiks works beautifully for the rocks. Use a variety of prints for your foliage area. This will make a more visually interesting composition.

Remember, everything gets more MUTED in color and grayer in value as it recedes towards the background. Choosing your fabrics accordingly will greatly enhance the sense of depth and perspective in your work.

Creating distance across a large body of water requires that you change the value or mood of the water as it recedes into the distance and approaches the horizon. I changed the water in the front bay to make it calmer and darker. You can achieve this effect by strip-piecing lighter and darker complementary water fabrics together. Another method is to appliqué strips of different fabrics together with gentle curves along the top edges as I have done. The easiest method of all is to use the fabric paint crayons (see the General Instructions, page 16). Overdye a darker color onto your lighter color water fabric as you come forward into the bay area.

Personalize your quilt by adding your own unique touches to the lighthouse design, beach, or rocky shore. Possibilities include a picnic blanket, the back of a bench, a cherished lighthouse decoration.

The sky is made using 2½" x 2½" squares. Place them in rows on-point and sew together. The contrast between geometric piecing and curvilinear appliquéd shapes is very dramatic. A pieced sky also enables you to add in sunrise colors or gradations of value. Note that the sky is lighter at the horizon line.

Fabrics Needed

- 5 - ⅛ yard cuts of light to medium blues or sky prints (Make sure that they don't have a strong directional pattern when set on-point.)
- ½ yard of water fabric OR ½ yard total of 2-3 different gradations of water fabrics
- 6" x 12" light gray or white and 6" x 12" red for the lighthouse wall. (I used Northcott Stonehenge white/gray for the tower.)
- Scraps of black for the lighthouse and guardhouse details
- 2" x 4" synthetic shiny sheer or silk organza for lighthouse window glass (Make sure you can iron it with a lower heat setting!)
- Tiny scraps of gray for the stone wall at the base of the lighthouse (You can use the same fabric that you will use in the fall and winter pattern.)
- 2" x 5" red for the guard house roof (Be sure it has enough contrast when placed next to the red stripes on the lighthouse.)
- 3" x 3" light gray for the lighter side of guard house (This print needs to be different from the gray used on the lighthouse.)

- 2" x 4" slightly darker gray for the shaded wall
- Scraps of black for under the eaves
- 2" x 5" gray for the sand
- 4" x 17" earth tone for the path
- 2" x 2" scrap white for the beach umbrella (Use a permanent blue marker or Inktense™ pencil for stripes.)
- ¼ yard batik, ombre or Stonehenge print for the rocks and breakwater rocks (Use both lighter and darker areas of value found in the same print.)
- 4" x 12" grassy lawn print for in front of lighthouse
- 2" x 6" light green for the distant breakwater
- Variety of small 3" x 4" scraps for the bushes
- Tiny scrap pieces for the sailboat OR fussy cut from preprinted fabric (Make sure your sail and boat have enough contrast against the water.)
- ¼ yard for the 1" inner border strips (Use a color that will help pop the colors used in the quilt interior.)
- ½ yard for the 2½" outer border strips (You may want to just increase the fabric used for the outer border strips.)
- ⅜ yard binding
- 1 yard of backing
- 1 yard of batting

Sewing Instructions

1. Trace your entire pattern onto a clear plastic overlay (page 10).

2. You need a total of 68 squares for a pieced sky. I fussy cut many of mine as I was trying to blend gradually into a new color or value. Find a part of the sky print that is a little darker and fussy cut to get part of that darker area into a predominately lighter square. That is how you make the gradual changes that blend together softly across your sky. For a pleasing visual effect, vary the value from darker at the top to lighter at the horizon. Cut out each square at a 90-degree angle OR you can cut 2½" strips from each of the different sky prints. (See what a sunset sky looks like on page 63.)

3. Arrange the squares on point. Use the grid on your pattern to audition them before sewing them together. There will be 12 rows across. Refer to your grid to see how many squares in the row. Sew the individual rows together. Then begin sewing rows in pairs. Add two rows together, then sew another two, and so on.

> *Sewing the strips together one-by-one to the next row can cause stretching and distortion if you have fussy cut any of them on the bias.*

Kathy McNeil · Landscape Quilts with Kathy

4. Trim the pieced sky to measure 12½" x 21½".

5. Cut the water fabric 11" x 21½" OR, to create more depth, consider appliquéing or piecing the water section with a gradation in value as described in Fabric Suggestions (page 31).

6. Sew the sky section to the water section. This will be your background. All other pictorial images will be placed on top.

> **The rock wall encircling the tower #16 needs to fall behind the tower and be darker in value.**

> **Make the whole lighthouse as a separate unit before placing it on the background.**

7. For the lighthouse tower, cut out the background tower wall base shape. Add the red stripes on top. Add the black window.

8. Make the lighthouse top floor. Add the black roof over the top floor.

9. Cut out the sheer window fabric in one piece, then add black strips over the sheer window fabric. Position in place between the top floor and the tower.

10. Cover both the top floor and tower edges with the red strips. Satin stitch in the little railing using a very narrow stitch width. Use tear-away stabilizer behind your sky when adding the satin stitching.

11. For the stone wall, be sure to place the dark back (inside) side wall behind the lighthouse. The front side and top edge should be in front of the lighthouse and behind the guard house.

12. Place the tree in position behind the guard house. (Mine was fussy cut from a great fabric find!)

13. Assemble the guardhouse as numbered. Add the black eaves and trim last and appliqué in position over the lighthouse. Trim away any part of the tower that is too bulky behind the guardhouse. Shade and darken the left and top in-side of windows with your paint crayons or Inktense™ pencils.

Tip

Shade and darken the left and top in-side of windows with your paint crayons or Inktense™ pencils.

14. Add the sandy beach. The sand should be grayer in color than the path fabric. Overlap the path fabric on top of the sand.

15. Build the rocky shore. Add the rocks as numbered. Be sure that shaded sides of rocks are darker in value. Add overlapping extensions to all the shapes that will have another piece fit on top. The hill, rocks, and bushes go on top of the sand and path. Optionally, shade the right side of the path with dark green tulle or fabric paint crayons. I slipped the tulle under the rocks and bushes along the right side and let it overhang on to path. Quilting held it in place.

16. Complete and add the beach umbrella.

17. Overlap the lawn over of the rock wall and guard house. It is part of the rocky shore top area.

18 Add the hill on the left. (You may use the same hill fabric from your Fall pattern). If your print does not have enough variety or the scale size is not right, just collage this area from the prints your do have.

19. Now complete the larger rock shapes that overlap the lawn (#39, #40, #43, and #44).

20. Complete overlapping tree and foreground bushes along the lower right side.

21. Add the rocky mid-ground breakwater. Use lighter colored rocks and grass to add more perspective.

22. Add the sailboat. Position it where you think it looks best in the water.

23. For turned edges, trim all background from behind pictorial elements.

Finishing

Square up and trim to measure 20½" x 22". Be sure to square parallel to the horizon.

For the inner border, cut two strips 1" x 22" and add to sides. Cut 2 strips 1" x 21½" and add to top and bottom. Trim as needed.

For the outer border, cut 2 strips 2½" x 23" and add to the sides. Cut 2 strips 2½" x 25½" and add to top and bottom.

Optional—add pictorial images or glued on shells to your border.

Quilting your Quilt

Layer the quilt top, batting, and backing and pin baste together about every 3".

Begin by outline quilting all the major shapes. Go back and quilt within the shapes, adding texture that will enhance the visual look of the image; for example, pebbling around the stones in your rock wall, adding a visually receding path to the pathway to the beach.

Be consistent with the density of your free-motion quilting across the entire quilt top.

Pattern sample for SUMMER. Full size pattern on CD.
Printed pattern must measure 22" x 20½". Please check your printed pattern before you begin.

Fall

FALL, 25½" x 27", made by the author
Used with permission from Falls Mill Museum, Belvidere, Tennessee, www.fallsmill.com

Kathy McNeil Landscape Quilts with Kathy McNeil

Fabric Suggestions

Use small-scale rock or brick fabrics for the two rock walls. Use a lighter fabric with enough contrast to make the water wheel stand out from what is behind it. Using multiple prints with slight differences in value will add dimension and form to your foliage, ground, and buildings. I used a fabric with gradations in value for the old red mill room in front of the house.

The tree foliage is the suggested outside shape. Smaller shapes can be placed together. Collage together your fall tree leaf clumps using a couple of different fall foliage prints.

Foreground bushes should be larger in scale and more saturated in color than the foliage in the middle area behind the house on the left. Remember, everything gets more MUTED in color and grayer in value as it recedes towards the background. Choose your fabrics accordingly.

Fabrics Needed

- ⅜ yard for the sky
- ⅜ yard muslin or lightweight interfacing
- 4 – 8" x 8" squares of fall foliage prints for the treetops
- ¼ yard gray-brown for the tree trunks
- 4-6 scraps of small-scale shrubbery prints for the landscaped bushes OR fussy cut from landscape panels
- 6" x 6" golden brown for the ground (The Northcott Stonehenge line of fabrics are great for ground and rocks.)
- ¼ yard gray print for the dark rocky hill under the house
- 9" x12" light brown/beige for the house
- 9" x 12" brick red brown for the mill shed and house roof (I used an ombre fabric and cut the boards from the darker area.)
- 9" x 9" light golden brown for the waterwheel
- 8" x 8" gray print for the rock wall support for the waterwheel
- 3" x 6" darker gray print for the shaded side of the rock wall support

- 1" x 1" scrap of black for the cog wheel circle center of the waterwheel
- Scraps of gray or brown for the rocks (Use a lighter value for the tops of the rocks.)
- 4" x 14" water for the pond
- 6" x 17" lawn or grass hill area (You can construct this area from smaller shapes and use multiple scraps.)
- ⅓ yard of lightweight interfacing or muslin
- ¼ yard stabilizer
- ¼ yard for the 1" inner border strips (Use a color that will help pop the colors used in the quilt interior.)
- ½ yard for the 2½" outer border strips
- ⅜ yard binding (You may want to just increase the fabric used for the outer border strips.)
- 1 yard of backing

Sewing Instructions

1. To create the background, cut a 12½" x 21" rectangle of sky fabric. Cut an 11" x 21" rectangle of muslin or light-weight interfacing. Join the pieces on the long side to make a 23" x 21" rectangle. The interfacing gives you a surface for fusing on the pictorial elements. For turned edges, trim all background from behind pictorial elements.

2. Trace the entire pattern onto a plastic overlay (page 10).

3. Appliqué the 3 designated tree/leaf foliage areas. Wait to place the tree trunks on top of the leaf foliage bushes and ground. Fussy cut smaller leaf shapes to go over some of the branches and trunk for a more realistic look. You may cut away and remove the parts of the trunk and branches that will lie under your fussy cut shape. Do not place the shapes that overlap the house and shed until house is in position later.

Quilts with Kathy McNeil

4. Add the bushes on left back, the ground, and the tree trunks now following the suggested numbered sequence.

5. Cut out the dark rocky hill under the house and wheel. See all the shaded speckled area on the pattern.

FALL

Be sure to add an extra extension underneath and behind the bottom board of the shed, and behind the house and wheel. Position in place. Appliqué.

6. Add rocks on left side. The top of the rocks should be lighter in value.

7. Make the house and mill shed as a separate unit. The old mill section can be made from one piece of fabric with the board strips layered on top. The boards should be ½" strips horizontally and ¼" strips vertically. The window trim is ¼". Machine appliqué the boards, window, and sills with a flat, narrow zigzag stitch. Be sure to use tear-away stabilizer when doing the machine appliqué. Add shading to the top and left side of the windows with paint crayons or Inktense pencils.

Kathy McNeil ❦ Landscape Quilts with Kathy McNeil

8. Place your house/mill into position. Appliqué in place.

9. Add the lower mid-level tree on the right. It should overlap the side of the house a bit. Place remaining leaf shapes in position that overlap the house.

10. Add the pond and the bush behind the wheel. Optionally, landscape little grasses or bushes over mill shed posts.

10. Add the spillway support rock wall and the dark brown water spillway on top of the larger wall (#16, #17, #18, #19, and #20).

There is an outside board connecting the spillway to the wheel support wall. This board should lie on top of the wheel. Mark slanted lines in the darker sides of the two support walls with a fine point permanent Sharpie. Quilt these lines in with a contrasting color of thread. I have put the lines in with a narrow zigzag stitch in white. Follow the corner angle in the pattern. These lines will help the perspective.

11. Cut out the wheel as one continuous piece. Add center hub metal-looking circles. Place in position and appliqué.

12. Add the wheel support wall in front of the water wheel (#26 and #27). The side should be darker in value. Add the perspective lines on the shaded side as described above.

13. Add the foreground bushes and grassy hill field following the suggested numbered sequence. Add more bushes if your hill print does not have multiple bushes.

14. Layer the final fall leaf foliage shapes that overlap the top of the house and the mill shed.

For the inner border, cut 2 strips 1" x 22" and add to the sides. Cut 2 strips 1" x 21½ and add to the top and bottom. Trim as needed.

For the outer border, cut 2 strips 2½" x 23 and add to the sides. Cut 2 strips 2½" x 25½ and add to the top and bottom.

Quilting your Quilt

Layer the quilt top, batting, and backing and pin baste together about every 3".

Finishing

Square up and trim to measure 20½" x 22".

Personalize your quilt by adding your own unique touches to the grassy field. Possibilities include a picnic blanket, the back of a bench, old farm equipment, pumpkins in the border, or a spinning wheel.

For turned edges, trim all sky background from behind pictorial elements.

Begin by outline quilting all the major shapes. Go back and quilt within the shapes, adding texture that will enhance the visual look of the image; for example, pebbling around the stones in your rock wall and adding texture to the tree trunks

Be consistent with the density of your free-motion quilting across the entire quilt top.

Pattern sample for FALL. Full size pattern on CD.
Printed pattern must measure 22" x 20½". Please check your printed pattern before you begin.

Winter

WINTER, 32½" x 25½", made by the author

Fabric Suggestions

Batiks with little print and whites with bits of gray or blue work great for snow. Use multiple prints for your snow area or paint in shaded snow fabrics with the fabric paint crayons. This will make a more pleasing and interesting composition. I used an ombre fabric with gradations for the red Christmas cabin. The side walls should be darker in value.

Remember, everything gets more MUTED in color and grayer in value as it recedes towards the background. (See the distant mountains on the right side as an example). Choose your fabrics accordingly.

The reflections in the river can be made with a combination of paint, slivers of fused moon fabric, and/or thread work. Stars in the sky were hand embroidered with metallic thread.

The shapes on the pattern are suggested shapes! They indicate the maximum size a snowbank should be. Collage your snowbank clumps together until they cover the approximate area shown in the pattern. The tree line is a suggested shape of a silhouette forest.

Fabrics Needed

- 28" x 8" royal blue for the sky
- ¼ yard of white-on-white (Do not use a sheer fabric)
- ¼ yard of batik white with some light blue, lavenders, or grays in it
- Optionally, you can always take good quality white cotton and paint in some colors with fabric paint crayons. Mix a dilute color in your mixing palette. Sponge paint the color onto your wet white cotton for wonderful shaded snow fabric.
- ¼ yard of medium bluish gray for the shaded sides of the mountain peaks
- ¼ yard of very light gray for the brighter side (Do not use a sheer fabric. You do not want shadow-through issues! Snow patches will be white-on-white on the brighter mountain side.)
- 3" x 20" medium gray-blue print for dark side of hill
- 9" x 21" lighter side of the hill (Use medium blue print similar in hue but lighter in value to dark side of the hill.)
- 6" x 6" yellow for the moon (Mine was a hand dye that had a white streak in center. Use for reflections also.)
- 3" x 3" dark blue with a print that is different from the hills for the rock left front
- ¼ yard black or navy blue near black for the dark silhouette trees and large tree trunks
- 9" x 20" dark blue print with swirls for larger trees OR ¼ yard of dark blue Christmas tree novelty print
- ¼ yard ombre fabric that goes from lighter to darker red for the cabin
- Use scraps from moon for windows.

- ¼ yard of light yellow for the road (Fairy Frost fabric with its sparkles works great.)
- ¼ yard of organza or separate blue print for the shadow on the road
- 6½" x 17" for the river (Use a dark inky blue batik with no discernible motif or a dark water print.)
- Scraps of black for smaller posts
- 2" x 6" dark green for the larger posts
- 5" x 10" for the bridge (A gray small scale rock wall fabric works well. You can repeat rock fabric from FALL or SUMMER.)
- Scrap of dark small scale print for the railing
- Dark red 30 or 40-wt. thread to satin stitch in railing detail
- Variegated 30-wt. blue thread for rope from post to post
- Use a satin stitch for both the railings and rope.
- 28" x 13" muslin or lightweight interfacing
- ⅜ yard inner border (Use a color that will help pop the colors used in the quilt interior.)
- ¼ yard EACH 4–5 navy blue or darker prints for a pieced outer border (optional) OR ⅜ yard navy blue or darker print (Some of the strips can be scraps from fabrics used inside the quilt.)
- ⅜ yard binding (You may want to just increase the fabric used for the outer border strips.)
- 1 yard backing
- 1 yard batting

Kathy McNeil · Landscape Quilts with Kathy McNeil

Sewing Instructions

1.Trace your entire pattern onto a clear plastic overlay (page 10).

2. Cut a 28" x 8½" rectangle of sky fabric and a 28" x 13½" rectangle of lightweight muslin or interfacing. Join to make a rectangle 28" x 22" for your background. The interfacing gives you a surface for fusing the pictorial elements in place.

3. Appliqué the moon to the sky.

4. Add the base mountain shapes using the numbers for the suggested layering sequence.

5. Add snow patches to mountains. The dark side of the snow patches should be lighter than the darker base fabric. Be sure to use white-on-white snow patches on lighter sides.

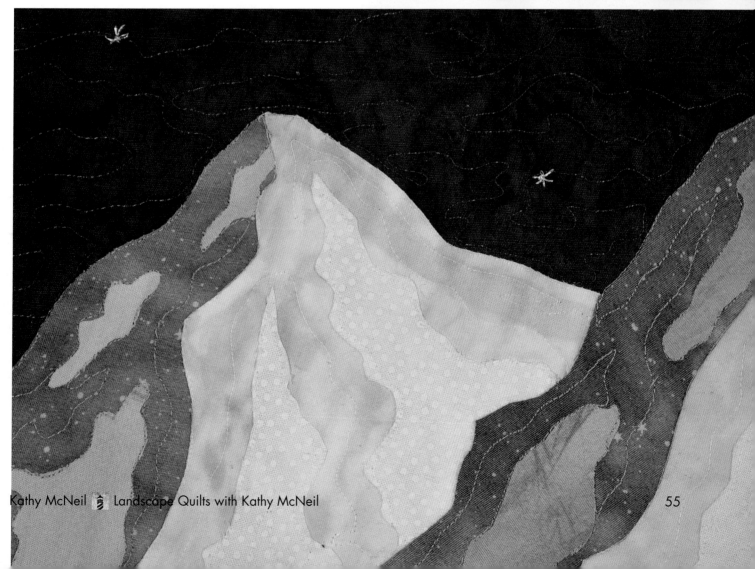

6. Add the hill, doing the darker shaded side first.

7. Add distant hills on the right with all the snow patches. These hills fall behind the lighter side of the large hill shape in the center front.

8. Layer the lighter side of large hill over the shaded side. Be sure to have enough overlap so that it will fall behind the dark tree line, behind the big tree trunks, and slightly under the cabin.

9. Add larger dark blue novelty print trees on either side.

10. Add the silhouette trees (#10 – #15). Note the suggested layering numbers. Partial black trees fall behind the other trees.

11. Add the shadowed darker gray snowbank (#17).

12. Add the dark green, rounder tree on the left side under the cabin.

13. Construct the cabin as a separate unit. Finish the entire building before positioning in place. Fussy cut from ombre fabric for lighter and shaded right sides. The little room in the front should be the lightest in value. Add the yellow windows. Place the cabin on tear-away stabilizer and satin stitch in the window frames. Add the snowy roof.

If you have shadow-through issues, add one more layer of lightweight stabilizer or white fabric behind the snowy roof.

14. Add the snowbanks in front of the cabin as numbered; #30 should be lightest and brightest.

15. The road in front of the house is next. First add all the smaller fence posts. The rope between posts is a satin stitched with variegated blue and white thread. Next, overlap the base of the posts with the road in front of the cabin.

16. Cut out the river, allowing enough of an extension to go under the bridge **and** under the snow fields on both sides.

17. Make the bridge with the shadowed undersides of the tunnels in the bridge. Use darker fabric or paint to add a shadow to the bridge fabric you are using.

18. The railing is a separate fabric piece that goes on top, following the contour of the bridge top. Satin stitch along the top and bottom edges with a dark red color of thread. Add vertical lines every ½". Gradually make the satin stitch wider as you approach the left side of the bridge to enhance perspective. Use tear-away stabilizer behind the background while satin stitching.

Kathy McNeil 🎨 Landscape Quilts with Kathy McNeil

19. Add the posts and snow tops.

20. Cut slivers of moon fabric for reflections in the water. Consider painting in some yellow ripples.

21. Add the snowbanks along the left side of the river.

22. For the road in the foreground, the top of the road tucks behind the bridge. Cut a slit in the road where it intersects with the tree. Add the tree and allow it to fall in front of the slit.

23. The rest of the road will fall on top of the snowbanks. Add a dark shape in road with sheer organza or blue fabric.

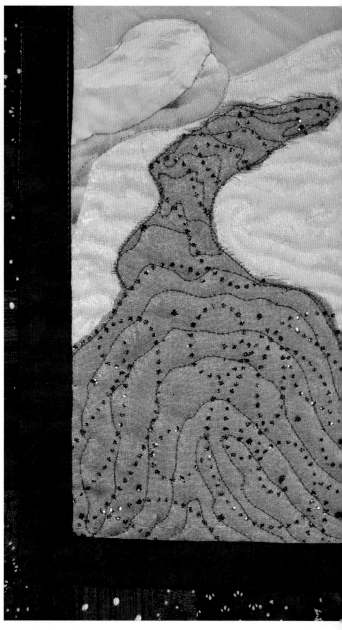

24. Complete all snowbanks and big trees on the right. Use a darker value print for the under sides of the snowbanks. Try to fussy cut out some variations in your white batik or prints to separate them visually from each other OR paint dilute colors into the snowbanks so they don't fall flat.

Finishing

Square up and trim to measure 27½" x 20½".

For turned edges, trim all background sky from behind pictorial elements.

For the inner border, cut 2 strips 1" x 20½" and add to the sides. Cut 2 strips 1" x 28½" and add to the top and bottom.

From a single dark outer border fabric, cut 2 strips 2½" x 21½" and add to the sides. Cut 2 strips 2½" x 32½" and add to the top and bottom.

Optionally, make a 2½" wide pieced border as follows:

- Cut the outer border yardage into multiple strips 3" x 1½".

- Sew strips together alternating the various prints as shown. You will need a completed pieced border section 3" x 21½" each side.

- Measure the width to verify exact measurements for top and bottom pieced border strips, 3" x 32½"

Quilting your Quilt

Layer the quilt top, batting, and backing and pin baste together about every 3".

Begin by outline quilting all the major shapes. Go back and quilt within the shapes, adding texture that will enhance the visual look of the image. For example, add contours to your snowbanks and mountains. Quilt over reflections in the water with yellow thread.

Be consistent with the density of your free-motion quilting across the entire quilt top.

Kathy McNeil   Landscape Quilts with Kathy McNeil

Pattern sample for WINTER. Full size pattern on CD.
Printed pattern must measure 27½" x 20½". Please check your printed pattern before you begin.

Resources

Visit my web store www.kathymcneilquilts.com for Apliquick®™ turned edge supplies, Caran d'Ache Neocolor™ II Artists' Crayons and my *Learning Landscapes* DVD.

The DVD has one hour and 55 minutes of instruction that includes:

Important design tips for landscapes
Choosing fabrics that create depth and dimension
Learning to shade and add highlights and form with my fabric paints
Turned- and raw-edge appliqué techniques
Tips on quilting the pictorial quilt

Look over my shoulder as I walk you through the construction of the seasonal patterns. The DVD includes tips for choosing fabrics, turned- and raw-edge appliqué techniques, assembling the four quilts, how to use fabric paint crayons for shading, and quilting landscape quilts.

I prefer using 5mm plastic laminate for the clear plastic positioning overlays. It lies flat, does not have static cling that can be a problem with vinyl, and it can be reused by wiping off the permanent marker with rubbing alcohol. It is available from office supply stores. Ask them to run you the size you need for your pattern. No, you don't need to laminate anything between the two layers of plastic; you just want the clear plastic.

Ginger's Needleworks (www.quiltknit.com) for landscape and architectural fabrics

You'll find sizing spray at Walmart® or your local grocer located right next to the spray starch.

Derwent™ Inktense™ pencils are available from art supply stores and online

About the Author

Meet Kathy McNeil

Photo by Bruce McNeil

Kathy McNeil is an internationally recognized award-winning quilt artist, judge, teacher, and designer. Sewing thousands of little scraps of fabric together by hand, she creates quilts that look like paintings. Her pictorial quilts are frequently featured in museums, magazines, calendars, and international shows. Many of her quilts are in private collections.

Her work is traditional in technique and realistic in style. Quilt tops begin as a sketch, which she enlarges to the size of the finished quilt. About 75 percent of the finished quilt will resemble the sketch as she works out each little area or character, listening to the fabric and how it can best reveal the heart and soul of the piece.

Hand appliqué is her technique of choice. All edges are turned under and appliquéd, usually, with silk thread. Kathy loves the rhythm and serenity it gives and the ease of being able to rip out when a new idea or inspiration carries her away. She teaches raw-edge, machine, and hand appliqué, hoping that each student will find the technique that best works for them. She plans to elaborate on her methods through online classes. These workshops have been created to build confidence with technical skills and creativity.

Describing herself as a "scrappy" quilter, she often uses over a hundred different fabrics in one composition. Quilters ask her if she has rooms full of fabric. Pictorial quilters use small amounts of many, many small-scale prints and batiks in their work. Kathy has a couple hundred fabrics but only buys them in fat quarters.

Despite winning so many awards she calls herself a very common quilter. "I would rather my husband buy me tickets to a quilt show than jewelry. Sometimes I buy fabrics that I forgot I already had. And someday I really will burst my bladder by refusing to 'get up and go' until I get this last section DONE!"

Animals and landscapes are her favorite subjects. Kathy says, "I don't make things that Mother Nature doesn't make." She gleefully makes every leaf, feather, and tree a little different shape and size. Like nature, there are **no** points to match, **no** shapes that have to align perfectly—just freedom to play with color, line, and shapes. And **no** one can deny Mother Nature's sense of humor when seeing a hedgehog.

Kathy was a critical care nurse for thirty-five years. She is passionate about the health benefits of creativity. "Think about how you feel after several hours of combining colors and fabrics, working away on a beautiful quilt that makes you so happy. While losing yourself in that creative project you started relaxing. You lowered your heart rate, you lowered your blood pressure, and some studies even suggest that your levels of serotonin rise, which is like taking an anti-depressant." That quiet and focused state of mind may reduce pain and does bolster your immune system. "Quilting is healthy" and she quilts about 50 hours a week!

BEACH WALKS, made by the author.

More AQS Books

This is only a small selection of the books available from the American Quilter's Society. AQS books are known worldwide for timely topics, clear writing, beautiful color photos, and accurate illustrations and patterns. The following books are available from your local bookseller, quilt shop, or public library.

#1696

#1421

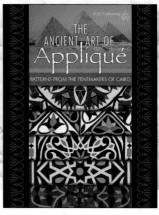

#1416

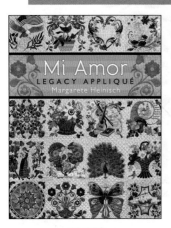

#1550

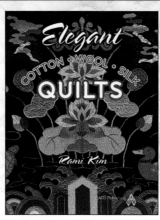

#8681

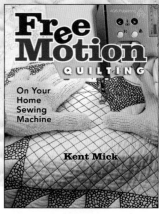

#1585

#1649

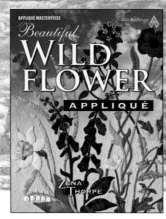

#8526

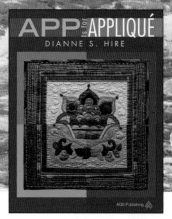

#1419

LOOK for these books nationally.
CALL or **VISIT** our website at

www.AmericanQuilter.com

1-800-626-5420